Over 100
Helpful Household
Hints

Salt

Christine Halvorson

 Publications International, Ltd.

Writer

Christine Halvorson is the author of *100s of Helpful Hints: Practical Uses for Arm & Hammer® Baking Soda* and *The Home Hints Calendar 2000;* she is coauthor of *Amazing Uses for Brand-Name Products* and *Clean & Simple: A Back-to-Basics Approach to Cleaning Your Home.* She is a frequent contributor to *The Old Farmer's Almanac* publications, including *Home Owner's Companion, Gardener's Companion,* and *Good Cook's Companion.* Christine works as a freelance writer from her home in Hancock, New Hampshire.

Recipes on pages 52–53, 55, and 60–62 are used with permission from the University of Minnesota Extension Service, www.extension.umn.edu.

The recipe on pages 58–59 is used with permission from Henry Holt and Company, LLC, from *The Thirteen Colonies Cookbook* by Mary Donovan, Amy Hatrak, Frances Mills, and Elizabeth Shull, © 1975 by Praeger Publishers, Inc.

Illustrations by Bot Roda.

ISBN-13: 978-1-4127-1538-6
ISBN-10: 1-4127-1538-5

Manufactured in China.

8 7 6 5 4 3 2 1

Contents

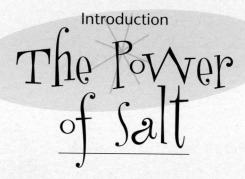

Introduction

The Power of Salt

From cleaning house to preserving food to helping soothe your aches and pains, salt can tackle even the toughest jobs. Once you start testing the solutions in this book, you will be amazed by the power of salt!

SALT'S STRENGTH

While there are dozens of ways to use salt at home, the most common industrial use is in making chemical compounds. Salt is key to the manufacture of steel, aluminum, rubber tires, soap, ceramics, textiles, and inks and dyes, not to mention thousands of medical applications. Once, mining or extracting salt was so complicated that salt was very expensive and people were often paid their wages in salt.

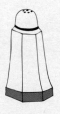

All animals, including human beings, require sodium for life and health, yet the human body cannot manufacture sodium on its own. When we lack salt, our muscles don't work properly, our food does not digest, and our blood circulation and heart are affected.

SOLUTION AFTER SOLUTION

The following pages offer more than 100 salt solutions for cleaning, cooking, preserving, and more. Before you know it, you'll become a salt expert. These are a few things you should know before you continue.

Whenever we mention *salt* we mean **regular table salt,** unless otherwise noted.

When a tip or recipe asks you to make a *paste,* mix a dry ingredient with a liquid ingredient to the consistency of toothpaste. Exact measurements are unimportant.

You will find sidebars throughout this book with tips ranging from how to make your copper pans sparkle to how to make doggie treats that can help control fleas. Also look for "Salt Snippets" for fun facts about salt.

Chapter 1

cleaning the Kitchen

Most people find that the kitchen is the most difficult room in their home to keep clean. And with good reason! With its endless supply of spills, drips, greasy pans, dirty dishes, and foot traffic, kitchen cleanup can certainly feel like an endless series of tasks. But thanks to salt, you don't need a different commercial cleaner to tackle each problem. An indispensable tool in any kitchen, this ingredient can clean practically anything plus perform some nifty restoration and maintenance tricks.

A+ SOLUTIONS FOR CLEANING APPLIANCES

Coffeemakers and coffee mugs

 Remove coffee and mineral stains from the glass pot of an automatic drip coffeemaker by adding 1 cup crushed ice, 1 tablespoon water, and 4 teaspoons salt to pot when it is at room temperature. Gently swirl mixture, rinse, and then wash as usual.

Remove tea or coffee stains from light-colored cups and mugs by rubbing stained areas with salt and a little water. Then wash as usual.

Ovens

If a pie or similar sugary item boils over in your oven, sprinkle the sticky spill with salt. Let it sit until spilled area becomes crisp, then lift off with a spatula when oven cools.

> **SALT SNIPPET**
>
> Salt was once a symbol of incorruption, and, therefore, making a covenant of salt was a binding agreement that was thought to last forever. For example, a passage from the Old Testament reads, "The Lord God of Israel gave the kingship . . . to David . . . by a covenant of salt" (2 Chronicles 13:5 NRSV).

Refrigerators

 To clean and refresh the inside of your refrigerator, sprinkle equal amounts salt and baking soda on a damp sponge, and wipe refrigerator surfaces.

Stoves

 Any spill on your stovetop can be cleaned up more easily if sprinkled with salt first. The mildly abrasive quality of salt removes stuck-on food, but it won't mar the surface.

Clean burned-on food from a stovetop burner by sprinkling it with a mixture of salt and cinnamon, then wipe away immediately. The mixture will give off a pleasant smell and cover up any burnt odor the next time you turn on the burner.

Soak up a liquid spill on a stovetop burner by sprinkling it with a mixture of salt and cinnamon. Leave it on spill for 5 minutes to absorb excess liquid, then wipe away.

CLEANING COOKWARE COULDN'T BE EASIER

Casserole dishes

 When you're faced with stubborn, baked-on food in a casserole dish, add boiling water and 3 tablespoons salt to dish. Let stand until water cools, then wash as usual.

Pots and pans

Get rid of excess grease in a roasting pan by first sprinkling it with salt. Then wipe pan with a damp sponge or paper towel, and wash as usual.

COPPER AS SHINY AS A NEW PENNY

Make your copper-bottom pans worthy of display. Sprinkle tarnished bottoms with salt, then scour stains away with a cloth dampened with vinegar. Rinse, then wash as usual. Another tarnish-fighting trick for copper pans: Use a spray bottle to apply undiluted vinegar to bottom of pan. Leave vinegar on pan until you can see tarnish evaporating. Next sprinkle vinegar with salt, and scrub entire surface with scrubbing sponge. Rinse, and repeat if necessary.

PRISTINE PIPES

Clogs

Help open up a slow-draining sink with a mixture of equal parts salt, vinegar, and baking soda. Pour solution down drain; let it sit 1 hour, then pour boiling or very hot tap water down drain.

A sink clog made up of greasy foods may be dislodged with ½ cup salt and ½ cup baking soda. Sprinkle this solution into drain, then flush with hot tap water.

Odors

Pour a solution of 1 cup salt and 2 cups hot water down kitchen drain to eliminate drain odors and break up grease deposits.

Pour ¼ cup each salt, baking soda, and dishwasher detergent into your garbage disposal. Turn on hot water, then run garbage disposal for a few seconds to clean out any debris and clear odors.

> ### SALT SNIPPET
>
> Some people consider spilling salt to be unlucky. This superstition dates back to at least the early days of Rome. In the painting "The Last Supper" by Leonardo da Vinci, Judas Iscariot, who betrayed Jesus to the authorities, is shown among the other disciples with a salt-cellar knocked over by his arm.

SPIFF UP KITCHEN ITEMS

Wood

 Clean a wood cutting board with soap and a little water. Follow cleaning by wiping board with a damp cloth dipped in salt until salt is gone. The salt treatment will leave the board looking and feeling fresh. (Never cut meat, poultry, or fish on a wood cutting board.)

 Wood breadboxes tend to become sticky with fingerprints and food. You can freshen one easily by wiping surface with vinegar on a sponge or cloth. Do this periodically to prevent grime buildup. A heavy buildup may require repeated wipes with a sponge dampened with vinegar and sprinkled with salt.

USEFUL UTENSILS THAT LOOK GREAT, TOO!

Silverware

 The tarnish on silverware can be removed by gently rubbing pieces with salt and a soft cloth and then washing them by hand with dish soap and warm water.

To clean sterling silver pieces and bring back their shine, rub them with a paste made of 2 tablespoons salt and ½ cup vinegar. Dip a clean, soft cloth in the paste, then gently rub silver pieces in a circular motion. Rinse, then dry with another soft cloth.

YOUR TABLEWARE NEVER LOOKED SO GOOD!

Dishes

When you can't wash the breakfast dishes immediately, sprinkle plates with salt to prevent any egg from sticking. This will make dishes easier to clean when you do have time.

ODOR EATERS

Plastic

Sprinkle some salt into a thermos or any closed container prone to developing odors. Leave overnight, then rinse. Smells should disappear, but repeat if necessary.

> **SALT SNIPPET**
>
> Ice cream makes its debut in Italy in 1559, as it's discovered that ice and salt make a freezing combination.

Chapter 2

House Cleanup

Are you ready to be awed by salt's ability to clean a carpet? Well, that's just the beginning! Salt is an extraordinary cleaning and deodorizing agent for your entire home. This chapter includes various recipes for homemade cleaning solutions that can hold their own against many of today's commercial products. So stock your cupboard with salt and get ready to tackle your home's toughest cleaning jobs.

MAKE YOUR BATHROOM BRIGHTER

Sinks

Make a paste of turpentine mixed with salt to restore white enameled fixtures that have gone yellow. Use this on sinks, bathtubs, or toilets. Apply, let sit 15 minutes, then wipe with a damp sponge.

MAGIC CARPET CLEANERS

Gravy

For a gravy stain on carpet, first remove as much liquid as possible by covering spot with salt. This will prevent the greasy stain from spreading. Then follow rug manufacturer's instructions. You may need a dry-cleaning solution or an enzyme detergent.

Grease

Try removing grease spots in a rug with a mixture of 1 part salt to 4 parts rubbing alcohol. Rub hard, going the same direction as the nap, then rinse with water.

Red wine

Immediately blot up all moisture from spill, then sprinkle area with salt. Let sit 15 minutes. The salt should absorb any remaining wine in the carpet (turning pink as a result). Then clean entire area with a mixture of ⅓ cup vinegar and ⅔ cup water.

REVITALIZE YOUR FURNITURE

Wicker

Keep white wicker furniture from yellowing by scrubbing it with a stiff brush moistened with saltwater. Scrub, then let piece dry in full sunlight.

Wood

When a hot dish or water has marred the surface of a wood table, get rid of the mark with a thin paste made of salad oil and salt. Just wipe on paste, then buff slightly as you wipe off with a soft cloth.

PEWTER CLEANER

Pewter must be cleaned gently because it is a soft metal that can be damaged easily. Follow this recipe to make a safe yet mildly abrasive paste.

Add flour to a mixture of 1 teaspoon salt and 1 cup vinegar until you can make a smooth paste. Apply paste to pewter piece. Allow to dry for a half hour, then rinse with warm water. Polish with a soft cloth, being careful to remove paste residue from all grooves or hidden areas.

WORKING WITH METAL

Brass and copper

 To clean and shine copper or brass surfaces, make a paste out of equal parts salt, flour, and vinegar. Rub on with a soft cloth, let sit about 1 hour, then wipe off and buff with a clean, soft cloth.

 Clean tarnish off copper decorative pieces by spraying them with vinegar and sprinkling with salt. Scrub pieces with a sponge, then rinse carefully, making sure to remove all salt traces. Repeat if necessary.

 Clean slightly tarnished brass or copper with a sliced lemon dipped in salt. Rinse.

Chapter 3

Around the Home

The chemical properties of salt make it useful for many common repair and maintenance jobs around the house. You can use salt to make your own plaster. Salt also does wonders at removing rust and stopping new candles from dripping. Salt can help in ways you never imagined!

WALL RECOVERY

Plaster

 Mix 2 tablespoons salt and 2 tablespoons cornstarch, then add enough water (about 5 teaspoons) to make a thick paste. Use paste to fill a small nail hole, chip, or other hole in Sheetrock™ or plaster. Let dry, then sand lightly and paint.

Do You Need Softer Water?

Sometimes household water can be too hard to do an effective job of cleaning. The water supply may contain high concentrations of the minerals calcium and magnesium because of the geology and source of water in that region. One way to determine if you have hard water is if your soap and laundry detergent don't lather very well or your glasses and dishes are left with significant water spots after running them through the dishwasher. Also, your bathtub and bath fixtures may develop a filmy feel.

A household water softener takes calcium and magnesium out of the water supply by using water softener salts, which are pellets of sodium that absorb the hardening minerals and keep the softener running efficiently.

HOUSEHOLD REPAIR HINTS AND TIPS

Candles

Stop new candles from dripping by first soaking them in a strong solution of ½ cup water and ½ cup salt for several hours. Let candles dry, then burn as usual.

> **SALT SNIPPET**
>
> Wit is the salt of conversation, not the food.
> —William Hazlitt

Fireplaces

An occasional handful of salt thrown into your fireplace fire will help loosen soot inside your chimney. It also makes a cheery, bright yellow flame.

Rust

Mix salt and cream of tartar, and moisten with enough water to make a paste. Apply to a rust stain on a piece of metal outdoor furniture; let sit in the sun until dry. Repeat if necessary.

Another rust removal method is to make a paste of lemon juice and salt. Apply paste to rusted object, and rub with a dry, soft cloth.

Chapter 4

Laundry Time

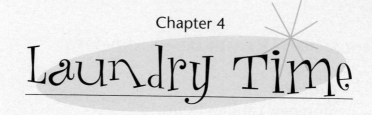

Salt is a super stain remover on clothing, helps maintain bright colors, and can even eliminate sticky spots on your iron. It can also reduce yellowing in clothes and mildew on shower curtains. Please note: None of the tips listed here should be tried with dry-clean-only fabrics.

THE BASICS

Color bleeding

 Add ½ cup salt to wash cycle to prevent new colored fabrics from running.

KEEP COLORS COLORFUL

Curtains and rugs

The colors of washable curtains or fiber rugs can be brightened by washing them in a saltwater solution.

Brighten faded rugs with a brisk rub using a cloth dampened with a strong saltwater solution.

THE PROBLEM OF PERSPIRATION

Don't sweat it. Those yellow stains in the armpits and around the collar of your favorite white T-shirts aren't a sign that you're sweating too much or not cleaning properly. These areas are just harder to get clean and are made up of more than just old perspiration and dirt. Undissolved deodorants may be a culprit, too. If you have hard water, the deodorant residue (and soap and perspiration) can't wash out properly. Below is a method for removing perspiration stains.

Mix 1 quart water with 4 tablespoons salt. Sponge this mixture onto stained area, then repeat until stain disappears. Wash as usual.

Yellowing

 Boil yellowed cotton or linen fabrics in a mixture of water, 1 tablespoon salt, and ¼ cup baking soda. Soak for 1 hour.

 Whiten nylon curtains by dissolving Epsom salt in warm water. Let soak 1 hour, then rinse with clear warm water, and hang to dry.

Ironing out the Rough Spots

Cleaning

An iron with rough or sticky spots on its surface can be cleaned by running it, set at low, over a piece of paper with salt on it.

Starch

Add a dash of salt to laundry starch to keep iron from sticking to clothing. This will also give a smooth finish to linens or fine cottons.

A Guide to Stain Removal

Blood

 Soak a bloodstain on cotton, linen, or other natural fiber in cold saltwater for 1 hour. Wash using warm water and laundry soap, then boil fabric in a large kettle of boiling water. Wash again.

A fresh bloodstain should disappear easily if it is immediately covered with salt and blotted with cold water. Keep adding fresh water and blotting until stain is gone.

Gravy

Try covering a fresh gravy stain with salt and letting it absorb as much of the grease as possible. A stubborn stain may need a 50/50 solution of ammonia and vinegar dabbed on and blotted until stain disappears.

Grease

Remove a fresh grease spot on fabric by covering it with salt. Wait for salt to absorb grease, then gently brush salt away. Repeat until spot is gone, then launder as usual.

Double-knit fabrics can be a stain challenge when it comes to grease. Add ½ teaspoon salt to a small dish of ammonia, and dab mixture directly onto grease spot. Let sit, then wash as usual.

Ink

Rub salt onto a fresh ink stain on fabric, and soak fabric overnight in milk. Wash as usual.

Mildew

Make a thin paste of lemon juice and salt, then spread paste on mildew stains. Lay clothing item out in the sun to bleach it, then rinse and dry.

A mixture of salt, vinegar, and water should remove mildew stains on most fabrics. Use up to full-strength vinegar if mildew is extensive.

Prevent mildew growth on shower curtains by soaking them in a bathtub full of saltwater (½ cup salt to the tub). Soak for several hours, then hang to dry.

RUST-REMOVING TREATMENT

Make a thin paste of salt and vinegar, then spread paste on rust stains in fabric. Lay item out in the sun to bleach it, or apply paste, stretch fabric over a large kettle, and pour boiling water through stained area. In both cases, allow item to dry, then check stain. Run item through rinse cycle in washing machine, then check stain again. Repeat treatment if any stain remains.

Wine

Remove a wine spill from cotton fabrics by immediately sprinkling stained area with enough salt to soak up liquid. Then soak fabric for 1 hour in cold water, and launder as usual.

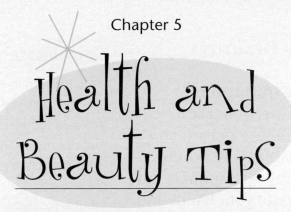

Chapter 5

Health and Beauty Tips

Salt solutions are wonderful—and inexpensive—additions to your beauty and stress-reduction regimens. Salt added to warm water can reduce dry and itchy skin, and salt and baking soda can be combined for a homemade mouthwash. Read on for even more beauty tips and tricks that will help you stay relaxed and beautiful without spending a fortune.

BODY BEAUTIFUL

Exfoliation

After you take a shower or bath and while your skin is still wet, sprinkle salt onto your hands and rub it gently all over your skin. This salt massage will remove dry skin and make your skin smoother to the touch. It will also invigorate your skin and get your circulation moving. Try it first thing in the morning to help wake up or after a period of physical exertion.

Itchy skin

Soaking in a tub of saltwater can be a great itchy skin reliever. Just add 1 cup table salt or sea salt to bath water. This solution will also soften skin and relax you.

TOOTHPASTE

A mixture of salt and baking soda makes an excellent toothpaste that can help whiten teeth and remove plaque, which contributes to cavities and gum disease. To make toothpaste, pulverize salt in a blender or food processor, or spread some on a cutting board and roll it with a pastry rolling pin to crush salt into a fine sandlike texture. Mix 1 part crushed salt with 2 parts baking soda, then dip a dampened toothbrush into mixture and brush teeth. Keep powder in an airtight container in your bathroom.

PUT ON A HAPPY FACE

Cleansers and toners

 Mix 1 teaspoon salt and 1 teaspoon olive oil in a small bowl, then use mixture to gently massage face and throat (being careful to avoid contact with eyes). Follow by washing with your usual face soap; rinse.

Oily skin

 To reduce oiliness, fill a small spray bottle with tepid water, add 1 teaspoon salt, and spray on your face. Blot dry.

FOR SWEET BREATH

Mouthwash

Mix ½ teaspoon salt and ½ teaspoon baking soda into a 4-ounce glass of water. Use this solution to gargle and freshen breath.

HELP YOUR HANDS

Odors

 To remove onion odor from your hands, sprinkle on a little salt, then moisten with a bit of vinegar. Rub hands together, and rinse.

Chapter 6

The Medicine Cabinet

Sore throats, toothaches, postnasal drip, bee stings, mosquito bites, painful gums, poison ivy, and poison oak are some of the ailments for which salt has been prescribed. Modern science doesn't endorse all of the traditional uses of salt, but this list offers a picture of the seemingly endless healing qualities salt may have.

It's Flu Season!

Sore throat

The simplest remedy for minor sore throat pain is a warm saltwater gargle (no matter how much you dislike the taste!). Just add 1 teaspoon salt to 8 ounces warm water, and gargle several times a day. See a physician if sore throat persists longer than 3 days or is accompanied by a high fever.

SALINE NOSE DROPS

Make your own saline drops to use for controlling annoying postnasal drip. People with sleep apnea, a condition that involves a dangerous interruption of breathing while asleep, may also want to try these drops to help keep nasal passages open.

Mix ¼ teaspoon salt and ¼ teaspoon baking soda into 8 ounces boiled water. Wait until mixture is room temperature, and draw liquid into an eyedropper, then apply to both nostrils with head tilted back. Hold this position for 15 seconds, then blow nose.

Add ¼ teaspoon salt and ¼ teaspoon baking soda to 8 ounces warm (not hot) water. Gargle with mixture 3 times a day to ease sore throat. If pain persists longer than 3 days, contact a physician.

ORAL DILEMMAS

Burns or injuries

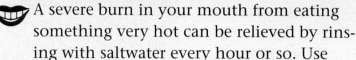 A severe burn in your mouth from eating something very hot can be relieved by rinsing with saltwater every hour or so. Use ½ teaspoon salt in 8 ounces warm water.

Biting the tongue or cheek can result in a large amount of blood but is rarely serious. To help ease the pain, rinse mouth with 1 teaspoon salt in 1 cup warm water.

Gums

Swish with 1 teaspoon salt in 4 ounces warm water when gums are painful. If you have an abscess, the salt will draw out some of the infection. Any gum pain should be treated by a dentist as soon as possible.

ALLERGY TREATMENT

Irrigating the nostrils and sinuses with saltwater is an excellent way to control persistent, annoying allergy symptoms. Dissolve ½ teaspoon salt in 8 ounces room temperature water. Draw mixture into a nose dropper, and inhale liquid through your nostrils. Repeat several times for each nostril, using 2 or 3 drops of solution each time. When through, blow nose until no discharge remains.

Toothaches

 As a temporary remedy for a toothache before going to the dentist, rinse your mouth with a mixture of 4 ounces warm water, 2 tablespoons vinegar, and 1 tablespoon salt.

WHEN SUMMER'S NOT FUN

Bee stings and bug bites

 Work a mixture of salt and water into a paste that will stick to a bee sting or bug bite. Apply paste; let sit until dry. This should relieve any itch or pain.

 Combine equal parts baking soda and salt, then brush onto a sting or bite area to help relieve itch.

Treat a mosquito bite by soaking it for a few minutes in saltwater, then applying an ointment made of salt and lard.

Poison ivy and poison oak

Help poison ivy clear up more quickly by soaking irritated skin in hot saltwater.

Chapter 7

Fun With Salt

Salt is an inexpensive ingredient for dozens of fun-filled arts and crafts projects for children and adults. What's more, salt can be used in tricks that people have been studying for hundreds of years. The ideas presented here are only a handful of the many exciting activities that are possible with salt. Please note: Some of the projects for children require adult supervision.

Draw out the Artist in You!

Salt Dough

One of the most common creative uses for salt is to make a dough that is similar to molding clay and some of the popular play clays. Best of all, salt dough is easy to make and economical! Give this recipe a try with your children on the next rainy day or during school break.

1 cup salt
4 cups all-purpose flour
    Medium bowl
1½ cups warm water
    Rolling pin
2 tablespoons vegetable oil*

Mix flour and salt together in bowl. Add water, then knead dough and roll out as you would cookie dough. Add a little bit of flour if dough gets too sticky to work with.

*Add vegetable oil to dough only if you intend to store it for use at a later time.

Salt Painting

This cool art project will take your children a couple of days to complete, but the results will be well worth the wait!

Clear self-adhesive vinyl
Scissors
Salt
Watercolors
Paintbrush
Construction paper
Glue
Coloring book (optional)

1. Cut self-adhesive vinyl into a size suitable for drawing a picture (8 × 10 inches is a good size). Peel backing from vinyl, then sprinkle entire sticky side with salt. Hold up vinyl, and gently shake off any excess salt. Let sit for 2 days.

2. Place sheet of vinyl, salty side up, on top of a coloring book picture to trace, or over a plain piece of paper to make an original drawing. Using a set of watercolors and a paintbrush, paint salty side of vinyl to make the drawing. Paint lightly; too much pressure could ruin the paintbrush. Let dry, then remove paper from underneath sheet of vinyl. Glue painted salt paper to a background piece of paper to make it sturdy. You can glue it either salty- or smooth-side up.

Gift Bath Salts
Save money on gifts by making your own fragrant bath salts. This is a great activity to do with your kids, too!

Large glass or metal mixing bowl
2 cups Epsom salt
1 cup sea salt, rock salt, or coarse salt
Food coloring
Metal spoon
¼ teaspoon glycerin
Essential oil for fragrance such as vanilla,
  citrus, or peppermint (optional)
Glass jars with screw-on metal lids or cork
  stoppers or clear gift bags

This project is best done on a day with low humidity, as the salt will absorb moisture in the air.

Combine salts in bowl, and mix well. Add food coloring, and stir with metal spoon until well blended. (Food coloring will stain plastic or wooden spoons.) Add glycerin and about 4 to 5 drops of essential oil; stir again. Adjust coloring if desired by adding more food coloring. Spoon colored salts into decorative glass jars or gift bags. Add a gift tag with instructions to use ⅓ to ½ cup of the salts in a bath.

Holiday Hoopla

A Tisket, a Tasket, a Salt Dough Bread Basket
This is a great activity for older children, and the end result can make a wonderful gift or holiday centerpiece.

7-inch glass bowl
Nonstick vegetable oil spray
Aluminum foil
Flour
Knife
Ruler
Pastry brush
Water
Cookie sheet
1 egg
Small bowl
Clear shellac or varnish

1. Make one batch of Salt Dough (see page 33). Set dough aside. Turn glass bowl upside down, and spray entire outside surface with nonstick spray. Cover sprayed areas with aluminum foil. Smooth foil, and tuck extra edges inside bowl.

2. Lightly flour a tabletop or breadboard, then roll salt dough into a rectangular shape 14 inches long, 6 inches wide, and about ⅛ inch thick. Next cut 8 strips, each ¾ inches wide by 14 inches long. Lay out 4 strips of dough horizontally on your work surface. Weave remaining 4 strips vertically over and under horizontal strips, working very carefully. Don't leave any spaces between strips.

3. Using a pastry brush, spread water over the points where dough strips overlap. This will help bind them together. Slide woven strip section to edge of tabletop, and hold bowl at counter level. Carefully slide strips onto bottom of the bowl. Overlap strips around edges of bowl and over each other. Press down in areas where strips bunch up.

4. Cut remaining dough into 3 strips, each ¾ inch wide by 26 inches long. Roll each strip into a rope shape. When you've created 3 ropes, braid them together into 1 rope. Place braided rope around rim of bowl on top of woven strips. Overlap ½ inch where the 2 ends of the braid meet, and press these overlapped parts together. Trim off any excess dough. Moisten braided rope and lattice dough strips where they overlap, and gently press them together a little more. Place dough-covered bowl on a cookie sheet, and bake at 325°F for 30 minutes.

5. Remove from oven, and carefully remove dough from glass bowl. Keeping it upside down, place dough basket back onto cookie sheet. Beat 1 egg with 1 teaspoon water in a small bowl, then brush egg mixture onto dough basket. Return to oven and bake another 15 minutes or until basket is dry and golden brown. Remove to a wire cooling rack, and cool completely. Then shellac or varnish basket inside and out. Let dry 24 hours.

Grow a Crystal Garden

Who said gardens are only made of flowers? This cool project is a sparkling alternative, and it's educational, too!

    6 tablespoons salt
    6 tablespoons liquid bluing (a laundry
        whitening product)
    6 tablespoons water
    1 tablespoon ammonia
      Medium bowl
      Small rocks or rock pieces
      Shallow bowl
      Food coloring
      Tray or breadboard (optional)

Mix salt, bluing, water, and ammonia in a medium-size bowl. Place rocks in a shallow bowl. Pour mixture over rocks, then drip food coloring on top of rocks. Crystals will grow in about 3 weeks. After that time, keep adding water and they'll continue to grow. Place bowl on a tray or breadboard if crystals begin to grow over edges of bowl.

Chapter 8

Outside the Home

We've already seen hundreds of uses for salt inside your home. Now learn about the many ways to use this wonderful ingredient outside, too! Salt is a great alternative to toxic chemicals for controlling weeds and pests in your yard. Beyond the garden, salt is an excellent deicer in winter climates, and it can work wonders with your outdoor maintenance projects.

GREAT GARDENING

Poison ivy

A strong solution of saltwater can kill an area infested with poison ivy plants. Mix 3 pounds salt with a gallon of soapy water. Apply to leaves and stems of poison ivy plants using a garden sprayer.

Weeds

Boil 1 quart water, then add 2 tablespoons salt and 5 tablespoons vinegar. While still hot, pour mixture directly onto weeds between cracks on sidewalks and driveways.

PEST PATROL

Ants

Ordinary table salt sprinkled in areas where ants congregate may help deter them.

Cabbageworms

Cabbageworms frequently attack garden cabbages, broccoli, and cauliflower. To control them, dust the leaves of these vegetables with a mixture of 1 cup flour and ½ cup salt. Use this dusting powder in the morning or evening when plants are damp with dew.

Moths

 Salt sprinkled directly on a moth will kill it.

Slugs

 You can kill slugs by sprinkling them with a heavy dose of salt. Wait 5 minutes, then sprinkle them again.

CAMPING GEAR

Canvas

Deodorize canvas bags or any bags that have developed a musty smell by sprinkling the inside with salt, zipping up the bag, and letting it sit overnight. Remove salt in the morning, and allow bag to air out.

> **SALT SNIPPET**
>
> When you set out "to eat a man's salt," you will partake in his hospitality. Among Arabic people, eating a man's salt created a sacred bond between the host and guest. No one who has eaten of another's salt should speak ill of him or treat him unkindly.

Rust

 Clean the rust from bike handlebars or tire rims by making a paste of 6 tablespoons salt and 2 tablespoons lemon juice. Apply paste to rusted areas with a dry cloth, then rub, rinse, and dry thoroughly.

CARE FOR YOUR CAR

Oil spills

 If you accidentally spill oil onto your garage floor, sprinkle salt on it and wait 15 minutes. The salt will help soak up some of the liquid and make cleaning easier.

Windshields

 Avoid frosted car windows on a cold morning by rubbing them in the evening with a sponge dipped in a saltwater solution. Use 2 tablespoons salt to 2 cups water.

 Fill a small cloth bag or folded scrap of cloth with salt, and hold securely closed. Dampen bag with water, then rub it on outside of windshield to keep snow and ice from adhering.

SALT SNIPPET

In 1930, citizens of India began a campaign against their British occupiers and their monopoly on salt production. Civil disobedience leader Mahatma Gandhi led people to the Arabian Sea, and they produced salt by evaporating seawater, a violation of British-imposed law.

Chapter 9

Pets and Animals

You might be surprised to learn that salt can combat a flea infestation in your home or help remove deposits from your fishbowl. It never hurts to know exactly what you're feeding your pets, so this chapter also includes some recipes for effective homemade treats that use salt. Your pets will thank you!

Household Pets

Cats and Dogs

 If you've had a flea infestation in your home, sprinkle carpet or rugs with salt to help kill any flea eggs. Let stand a few hours, then vacuum. Repeat weekly for 6 weeks.

Put salt in your vacuum cleaner bag to help kill flea eggs that may have been vacuumed.

Flea-Be-Gone Dog Treats

Frugal dog owners can make a batch of homemade biscuits as treats. They will keep for weeks, are cheaper than store-bought varieties, and can even help control fleas. A batch of these would make a great gift for any dog lover.

Stir 3 tablespoons vegetable oil and 1 tablespoon garlic powder together in a large mixing bowl. In another bowl, mix 2 cups flour, ½ cup wheat germ, ½ cup brewer's yeast, and 1 teaspoon salt. Slowly add oil and garlic mixture to dry ingredients, and stir in 1 cup chicken broth when mixture gets too dry. Mix thoroughly until you get a doughy consistency. Roll dough onto a floured surface to about ¼ inch thick. Use knife to cut dough into squares, or, for a special treat, use cookie cutters to make dough shapes. Place shapes onto a large, greased baking sheet, and bake at 350°F for 20 to 25 minutes or until edges are brown. Allow to cool 2 hours, then store in plastic bags in a location dogs can't reach.

FIBER FOR FIDO

The bran in this doggie treat recipe will provide your pet with much-needed fiber.

In a very large mixing bowl, combine 2 tablespoons wheat germ, ¼ cup crushed bran flakes, 1 cup whole wheat flour, ⅛ cup cornmeal, ⅛ cup white flour, 1 tablespoon molasses, 2 tablespoons vegetable shortening, 1 teaspoon sage, 1 bouillon cube dissolved in ⅓ cup warm water, and 1 teaspoon salt.

Pour small batches of mixture into food processor and blend, adding water as mixture balls up. When it becomes 1 ball of dough, flatten and roll it onto a breadboard. Cut shapes out of dough with a cookie cutter or knife. Lightly grease a cookie sheet, and bake treats for 30 minutes at 350°F. Cool, and store in an airtight container.

Fish

Rub the inside glass of a fish tank with plain, noniodized salt. Use a plastic pot scrubber to remove hard-water deposits or other buildup. Rinse well before returning fish to tank.

Give your goldfish a little swim in saltwater for a change of pace and to perk them up. Add 1 teaspoon salt to a quart of freshwater, and let fish swim for 15 minutes. Then return them to normal conditions.

Chapter 10

Cooking Tricks

When it comes to cooking, salt has more jobs to do than just appearing as ingredients in recipes. It can perform miraculous tricks for improving flavor, preserving food, filling in for missing ingredients, and even making food look better. This ingredient can prevent spoilage and salvage the occasional cooking disaster. In fact, adding a pinch here and there during the preparation process may change the whole personality of certain foods.

COOKING TRICKS

Dairy products

Add a pinch of salt to any plain or mild-flavored yogurt to give it extra zing.

Fish and seafood

Freshen up fish just brought home from the market by returning it to its natural environment for a short time. Add 1 tablespoon sea salt to 2 quarts cold water, then add a lot of ice cubes. Soak fish in this saltwater for about 15 minutes, then remove it and dry it off before preparing as desired.

To get a good grip on a fish while trying to skin it for cooking, sprinkle your hands with a little salt.

HERBAL SALTS

Create herbal salts and store them with your spices to use in soups and stews or vegetable, chicken, and fish dishes.

Chop a handful of fresh herb leaves, then add 1 cup of salt. Crush salt/herb mixture with a mortar and pestle, or put in a blender and chop for 5 to 10 minutes. Spread mixture onto a cookie sheet in a shallow layer. Heat oven to 200°F. Bake 40 to 60 minutes, stirring frequently to break up any lumps. Remove from oven and allow to cool. Store herbal salts in a sealed jar away from heat and direct sunlight.

Fruits and vegetables

 To poach asparagus, add salt to water, and simmer exactly 5 minutes. Stalks should all be pointing in the same direction. (Some culinary experts insist the asparagus sit upright in the boiling pot.)

 Use up the usually unusable portions of broccoli stalks by cutting them into 1-inch-thick slices. Stir-fry them with salt, and eat as a snack.

After cutting hot chili peppers, be sure to scrub your hands and nails with soapy water. Then soak them in saltwater, and rinse. This will prevent the stinging chili oil from getting in your eyes.

PRESERVING HERBS

You can preserve herbs with salt. Just spread a thin layer of kosher salt in an airtight, rectangular container. Layer fresh herbs over salt (works best with basil, sage, or mint). Spread another thin layer of salt over herbs, then repeat layering process. Cover and store with your spices. To use, remove salt to expose herbs. Some may be darkened, but their flavor will be fine.

Meat

Salt will force juices out of meat and prevent it from browning. Wait to salt meat until midway through the cooking process, then salt it lightly. Or, wait until cooking is complete, then salt to taste.

Pasta

Adding salt to cooking water is a good idea, but wait until water boils. Then add 2 tablespoons salt for each pound of pasta. If you salt the water prior to boiling, it will take longer to boil.

Seasoning

Sprinkle peeled garlic cloves with a little coarse salt before attempting to chop them. The salt will absorb the garlic's juice and then dissolve, which will help spread garlic flavor further.

FOOD CLEANERS

Fruits and vegetables

Salt can help remove the gritty dirt that comes with some fresh vegetables. When washing arugula, leeks, or spinach, trim them first, then place them in a bowl of lukewarm water. Add a tablespoon of kosher salt, swish, and let vegetables soak for 20 to 30 minutes. Transfer vegetables to a colander, and rinse thoroughly.

Chapter 11

Recipes

Can you imagine life without salt? Many of our foods wouldn't be quite as flavorful, and some of them would spoil before you could even eat them! Salt shows up in many recipes, often to draw out the flavor of certain ingredients. Read on for just a sampling of the dozens of recipes that rely on this powerful ingredient.

MAIN DISHES

Jamaican Baby Back Ribs

   2 tablespoons sugar
   2 tablespoons fresh lemon juice
   1 tablespoon salt
   1 tablespoon vegetable oil
   2 teaspoons black pepper
   2 teaspoons dried thyme leaves, crushed
   ¾ teaspoon each ground cinnamon, nutmeg,
      and allspice
   ½ teaspoon ground red pepper
   6 pounds well-trimmed pork baby back ribs,
      cut into 3- to 4-rib portions
      Barbecue sauce

1. For seasoning rub, combine all ingredients except ribs and barbecue sauce in small bowl; stir well. Spread over all surfaces of ribs; press with fingertips so mixture adheres to ribs. Cover; refrigerate overnight.

2. Prepare grill for indirect cooking.

3. Baste ribs generously with your favorite barbecue sauce; grill 30 minutes more or until ribs are tender and browned, turning occasionally.

Makes 6 servings

SIDE DISHES

Cheesy Onion Flatbread

½ cup plus 3 tablespoons honey, divided
2⅓ cups warm water (105° to 115°F), divided
1½ packages active dry yeast
6 tablespoons olive oil, divided
3 cups whole wheat flour
⅓ cup cornmeal
4½ teaspoons coarse salt
3 to 4 cups all-purpose flour, divided
1 large red onion, thinly sliced
1 cup red wine vinegar
Additional cornmeal
1 cup grated Parmesan cheese
½ teaspoon onion salt
Black pepper to taste

1. Place 3 tablespoons honey in large bowl. Pour ⅓ cup water over honey. Do not stir. Sprinkle yeast over water. Let stand about 15 minutes until bubbly. Add remaining 2 cups water, 3 tablespoons olive oil, whole wheat flour, and cornmeal. Mix until well blended. Stir in salt and 2 cups all-purpose flour.

SALT SNIPPET

Our word *salary,* the pay we receive from employers, originated during the Roman empire when soldiers and civil servants were paid with rations of salt and other necessities. Together any such rations were referred to as salt.

Gradually stir in enough remaining flour until mixture clings to side of bowl.

2. Turn dough out onto lightly floured surface. Knead in enough remaining flour to make a smooth and satiny dough, about 10 minutes. Divide dough in half. Place each half in large, lightly greased bowl; turn over to grease surface. Cover; let rise in warm place (80° to 85°F) until doubled.

3. Meanwhile, combine onion, vinegar, and remaining ½ cup honey. Marinate at room temperature at least 1 hour.

4. Grease two 12-inch pizza pans; sprinkle each with additional cornmeal. Stretch dough and pat into pans; create valleys with fingertips. Cover; let rise in warm place until doubled, about 1 hour.

5. Preheat oven to 400°F. Drain onion; scatter over dough. Sprinkle with remaining 3 tablespoons olive oil, cheese, and onion salt. Season with pepper.

6. Bake 25 to 30 minutes or until flatbread is crusty and golden. Cut each flatbread into 8 wedges. Best served warm.

Makes 2 flatbreads, 8 wedges each

SALADS

Jalapeño Coleslaw

6 cups preshredded cabbage or coleslaw mix
2 tomatoes, seeded and chopped
6 green onions, coarsely chopped
2 jalapeño peppers, finely chopped*
¼ cup cider vinegar
3 tablespoons honey
1 teaspoon salt

*For a milder coleslaw, discard seeds and veins when chopping the jalapeños. Jalapeño peppers can sting and irritate the skin; wear rubber or plastic gloves
when handling peppers and do not touch eyes. Wash hands after handling.

1. Combine cabbage, tomatoes, onions, jalapeños, vinegar, honey, and salt in serving bowl; mix well. Cover; refrigerate at least 2 hours.

2. Stir well before serving.

Makes 4 side-dish servings

Marinated Green Beans and Potato Salad

1 pound fresh green beans, washed and
    trimmed
4 cups red potatoes, cubed and unpeeled
¼ cup red wine vinegar
2 tablespoons olive oil
2 tablespoons fresh lemon juice

BOILING WATER BATH

A boiling water bath helps kill bacteria during the canning process. To do this, place your canner on the stove and fill it a little over halfway with water. Set to boil. Load filled jars, fitted with lids and rings, onto canner rack. Add enough boiling water so water level is at least 1 inch above jar tops. Turn heat to its highest position until water boils vigorously. Then set a timer for the minutes indicated on recipe. Cover canner, and lower heat to maintain a gentle boil throughout processing time. If needed, add more boiling water to keep water level above jars. When jars have been boiled for the recommended time, turn off heat and remove canner lid. Set jars on a towel or cooling rack, leaving at least an inch between each jar.

4 cloves garlic, crushed
2 teaspoons honey
1 teaspoon salt
1 teaspoon dried dill weed
1 teaspoon dried thyme
½ teaspoon black pepper
4 cups ready-to-use fresh spinach, torn into
     bite-size pieces
1 medium tomato, cut into wedges

1. Bring 4 quarts water to a boil in Dutch oven. Add green beans; reduce heat to medium and cook, covered, 8 minutes or until beans are crisp-tender. Remove beans with slotted spoon.

2. Add potatoes to same Dutch oven. Cook, covered, 12 to 15 minutes or until potatoes are tender. Drain.

3. Combine vinegar, oil, lemon juice, garlic, honey, salt, dill weed, thyme, and pepper in medium bowl; whisk to combine. Add green beans and potatoes; stir to combine. Cover and refrigerate for up to 8 hours, stirring occasionally.

4. To complete recipe, arrange spinach on serving platter. Spoon green bean mixture over spinach. Pour remaining marinade over top. Garnish with tomato wedges.

Makes 6 servings

DRESSINGS

Chicken Salad Dressing
½ cup chicken stock
½ cup vinegar
5 egg yolks, slightly beaten
2 tablespoons mixed mustard
1 teaspoon salt
¼ teaspoon pepper
Few grains of cayenne
½ cup thick cream
⅓ cup melted butter

Combine first seven ingredients. Cook over boiling water, stirring constantly until mixture thickens. Strain, add cream and melted butter, then cool.

Makes about 2½ cups

Garlic Dressing
   ¾ cup olive or vegetable oil
   ¼ cup white wine vinegar
   1 clove garlic, pressed
   1 teaspoon salt
   ½ teaspoon black pepper

Mix all ingredients in tightly covered jar. (Dressing can be refrigerated up to 2 weeks.)

Makes 1 cup

French Dressing
   4 tablespoons olive oil
   2 tablespoons vinegar
   ½ teaspoon salt
   ¼ teaspoon pepper
      Few drops lemon juice (optional)

Put ingredients in small jar and shake. You may want to add a few drops of lemon juice for extra flavor.

Makes about ⅓ cup

Sauces and Dips

Creamy Cucumber-Yogurt Dip

　1 cucumber, peeled, seeded, and finely chopped
　　Salt
　¼ cup chopped fresh chives, divided
　1 package (8 ounces) cream cheese, softened
　¼ cup plain yogurt
　1 tablespoon fresh lemon juice
　1½ teaspoons dried mint
　　Black pepper
　　Assorted vegetables, chopped

1. Lightly salt cucumber in small bowl; toss. Refrigerate 1 hour. Drain cucumber; dry on paper towels. Set aside.

2. Reserve 1 tablespoon chives for garnish. Place remaining 3 tablespoons chives, cream cheese, yogurt, lemon juice, mint, and pepper in food processor or blender; process until smooth. Stir in cucumber. Cover and refrigerate 1 hour. Spoon dip into glass bowl or gift container; sprinkle reserved chives over top. Cover and store up to 2 days in refrigerator. Stir before serving with vegetables.

Makes about 2 cups

CONDIMENTS

Pineapple Chutney
2 pounds fresh
pineapple or 1 can
crushed pineapple
(1 pound 13 ounces)
2⅓ cups brown sugar
1 cup cider vinegar
1 cup dates, diced
1 cup raisins
1 cup sliced almonds
1 tablespoon minced onion
1 teaspoon salt
½ teaspoon ground cloves
½ teaspoon cinnamon
½ teaspoon ground allspice
¼ teaspoon garlic powder
⅛ teaspoon pepper

Mix all ingredients and cook over low heat for 1 hour or until very thick. Stir occasionally to prevent sticking. Seal in preserve glasses, or store in a large crock.

Potato Mayonnaise
1 very small baked potato
1 teaspoon salt
1 teaspoon powdered sugar
1 teaspoon mustard

> **SALT SNIPPET**
>
> A man must eat a peck of salt with his friend, before he knows him.
>
> —Miguel de Cervantes

2 tablespoons vinegar, divided
¾ cup olive oil

Remove skin and mash potato. Add salt, powdered sugar, and mustard. Then add 1 tablespoon vinegar, and press mixture through a fine sieve. Slowly add oil and remaining vinegar.

Makes about 1 cup

PICKLED FOOD

Dill Pickles
Use the following quantities for each gallon capacity of your container:

4 pounds pickling cucumbers, 4 inches each
2 tablespoons dill seed or 4 to 5 bunches fresh or dry dill weed, divided
2 cloves garlic, divided (optional)
2 dried red peppers, divided (optional)
2 teaspoons whole mixed pickling spices, divided (optional)
½ cup salt
¼ cup vinegar (5 percent)
8 cups water

1. Wash cucumbers. Cut ¹⁄₁₆-inch slice off blossom end and discard. Leave ¼ inch of stem attached. Place half of dill and spices on bottom of a clean container. Add cucumbers and remaining dill and spices. Dissolve salt in vinegar and water, and

pour mixture over cucumbers. Add suitable cover and weight to keep cucumbers below surface. Store where temperature is between 70° and 75°F for about 3 to 4 weeks while fermenting. Temperatures of 55° to 65°F are acceptable, but the fermentation will take 5 to 6 weeks. Avoid temperatures above 80°F, or pickles will become too soft during fermentation. Fermenting pickles cure slowly. Check container several times a week, and promptly remove surface scum or mold. Caution: If pickles become soft, slimy, or develop a disagreeable odor, discard them.

2. Fully fermented pickles may be stored in their original containers for about 4 to 6 months, provided they are refrigerated and surface scum and molds are removed regularly. Canning fully fermented pickles is a better way to store them. To can them, pour brine into a pan, heat slowly to a boil, and simmer 5 minutes. Filter brine through paper coffee filters to reduce cloudiness, if desired. Fill jars with pickles and hot brine, leaving a ½-inch headspace. Adjust lids and process in boiling water bath—15 minutes for pints, 20 minutes for quarts (see page 55).

Sweet Gherkin Pickles
    7 pounds cucumbers, 1½ inches or less
    8 cups sugar, divided
    6 cups vinegar (5 percent), divided

¾ teaspoon turmeric
2 cinnamon sticks
½ cup canning or pickling salt
2 teaspoons celery seed
2 teaspoons whole mixed pickling spice
½ teaspoon fennel (optional)
2 teaspoons vanilla (optional)

1. Wash cucumbers. Cut $\frac{1}{16}$-inch slice off blossom end and discard, but leave ¼ inch of stem attached. Place cucumbers in large container, and cover with boiling water. Six to 8 hours later, drain and cover with fresh boiling water; repeat on the second day.

2. On the third day, drain and prick cucumbers with a table fork. Combine 3 cups sugar, 3 cups vinegar, turmeric, and spices. Bring to a boil, then pour mixture over cucumbers. Six to 8 hours later, drain and save the pickling syrup. Add another 2 cups each of sugar and vinegar, and reheat to a boil. Pour over pickles.

3. On the fourth day, drain and save syrup. Add another 2 cups sugar and 1 cup vinegar. Heat to a boil, and pour over pickles. Six to 8 hours later, drain and save pickling syrup. Add 1 cup sugar and vanilla, and heat to a boil. Fill sterile pint jars* with pickles and cover with hot syrup,

leaving a ½-inch headspace. Adjust lids and process in boiling water bath for 10 minutes.

Makes 6 to 7 pints

To sterilize empty jars, put them right-side up on the rack in a boiling water canner. Fill canner and jars with hot (not boiling) water to 1 inch above tops of jars. Boil 11 minutes. Remove and drain hot sterilized jars one at a time.

CANDIES AND DESSERTS

Vanilla Ice Cream
2½ cups cold whipping cream
1½ cups cold milk
¾ cup sugar
1½ teaspoons vanilla
⅛ teaspoon table salt
Crushed ice
Rock salt

> **SALT SNIPPET**
>
> Eating too much salt may be contributing to bags under your eyes. Fluid retention in the body, a consequence of too much salt, can result in swollen eyes.

1. Combine whipping cream, milk, sugar, vanilla, and table salt in medium bowl; mix well. Pour mixture into freezer container of ice cream maker. (Do not fill freezer container to top; leave at least 2 inches of headspace above cream mixture to allow room for expansion when mixtures freezes.)

2. Follow manufacturer's directions for assembling ice cream maker. Fill ice cream maker with mixture of 8 parts crushed ice and 1 part rock salt

(or follow manufacturer's directions) to a level above the line of the mixture in the freezer container. Pack ice mixture firmly; let stand 5 minutes.

3. Follow the manufacturer's directions for freezing ice cream.

4. To harden ice cream, remove dasher; seal freezer container. Drain off ice mixture; repack ice cream maker with 3 parts crushed ice and 1 part rock salt. Let stand for 1 to 2 hours.

Makes 1½ quarts

Butter Taffy

   2 cups light brown sugar
   ¼ cup molasses
   2 tablespoons water
   2 tablespoons vinegar
   ⅞ teaspoon salt
   ¼ cup butter
   2 teaspoons vanilla

Boil first 5 ingredients until a small amount of mixture dropped in cold water becomes brittle. When nearly done, add butter and, just before turning into pan, vanilla. Cool, and mark in squares.